# Hard Skills Get You Hired But Soft Skills Get You Promoted

Learn How These 11 Must-Have Soft Skills Can Accelerate Your Career Growth

By

## Torquil Johners

# TABLE OF CONTENTS

***In all industries, organizations, and professions, soft skills are extremely valuable.***

Employers look for these abilities and attribute just as hard or technical skills since they help you be a productive and communicative team member. Understanding soft skills can assist you in identifying and improving your own, allowing you to be a more well-rounded applicant and employee.

To improve your career and achieve your goals in today's modern workplace, you must develop and demonstrate your soft skills. Different occupations necessitate different levels of hard skill proficiency. Coding, writing, and knowledge of certain computer applications are examples of these skills.

On the other side, soft skills are just as vital as hard skills; however, they are often overlooked. These intangible traits increase your productivity and make you have a favorable effect in the workplace. Soft skills are part of who you are for many people, but they can be cultivated and nurtured over time.

***So what are the most important soft skills, and what role do they play in your progress?***

To answer this and many other questions, we have designed this book. This book target the eleven most crucial soft skills for professional advancement in any industry.

To meet the aim, the book summarizes:

- ✓ Concept of Career Growth
- ✓ What exactly are soft skills
- ✓ 11 soft skills
- ✓ Communication
- ✓ Persuasion
- ✓ Negotiation
- ✓ Relationship Building
- ✓ Empathy
- ✓ Teamwork
- ✓ Positive Attitude
- ✓ Work ethics
- ✓ Time Management
- ✓ Conflict Resolution

and

- ✓ Emotional Intelligence

You may have a reputation as the best coder, editor, mechanic, or anything, but it means nothing if you don't get along with others. Some of the most crucial professional skills for both employees and employers simply cannot be taught or measured in a classroom. Soft skills are these characteristics, and they're more important to your job hunt and entire career than you might believe.

Non-technical talents that encourage productivity, efficiency and successful communication in the workplace are known as soft skills. Some soft talents are ingrained in your personality or are part of your work ethic. These abilities are frequently transferable across professions and industries, and they are required at all levels of the workplace, from entry-level positions to executive positions.

While your technical skills may get you in the door, it's your interpersonal skills that will open the majority of the doors. The soft skills that are critical for employment success include your work ethic, attitude, communication skills, emotional intelligence, and a variety of other personal characteristics.

You can succeed as a leader if you have these soft skills. If you have good soft skills, problem-solving, delegation, motivation, and team building become much easier. It's critical to know how to get along with others and keep a positive attitude if you want to be successful.

The difficulty is that the significance of these soft skills is frequently underestimated. They receive significantly less training than hard skills. The reason is organizations appear to expect employees to know how to behave at work for some reason.

They presume that everyone understands the value of being on time, taking the initiative, being friendly, and generating high-quality work but assuming that soft skills are ubiquitous is a recipe for disaster. That's why soft skills training and development are just as vital as traditional hard

skills training and development.

The process of choosing a career, enhancing your abilities, and progressing along a career path is known as career development. It's a lifelong learning and decision-making process that helps you get closer to your dream job, skillset, and lifestyle.

## CONCEPT OF CAREER GROWTH

Career growth is a set of actions or a continuous/lifelong process of advancing one's career, which includes setting new goals on a regular basis and learning new skills to achieve them. In an intra-organizational or inter-organizational setting, career growth usually refers to controlling one's career. It entails learning new skills, progressing to higher levels of responsibility, changing careers within the same company, relocating to a different company, or starting one's own business.

With the help of career growth, when someone is concerned about their professional growth, they identify their own strengths and weaknesses and then work hard to better their abilities. It also entailed learning about other professions and industries in order to find one that matched their skills, looking for possibilities to grow, and possibly changing occupations altogether if they found a more fit one.

# In a person's overall professional growth, there are several steps or stages:

### 1. SELF-EVALUATION

The first step in career development is self-assessment, which entails determining what type of career and growth one desires and what skills and interests one possesses.

### 2. AWARENESS OF CAREER OPPORTUNITIES

This is the stage in which a person investigates several job options that are in line with the self-assessment completed in the first step. Career awareness refers to a person's ability to investigate numerous domains and sorts of jobs/work that are available.

## 3. SETTING OBJECTIVES

This is the most crucial step in career development because it is here that one outlines specific short and long-term goals in order to achieve the desired profession. To begin, both short and long-term objectives must be defined.

Short-term team goals are more actionable, but long-term goals can be altered or changed as the company grows.

## 4. SKILL DEVELOPMENT

After deciding on a vocation and setting goals, one must acquire the necessary abilities to advance. Self-training or enrolling in a structured online or offline training program are also options for skill development. Once the necessary talents have been gained, the final stage can begin.

## SO, WHAT EXACTLY ARE SOFT SKILLS?

Soft skills are personal characteristics that are important for success and job advancement. They are often tied to how you work and interact with others.

Soft skills make it easier to develop relationships with others, making you more visible for the right reasons and opening up more job options for you.

You'll need soft skills regardless of where you work or what job you have. For many people, developing soft skills is the most challenging task.

## IS THERE A SOFT SKILLS GAP IN YOUR ORGANIZATION?

You have a soft skills gap when your staff has a lot of technical talents but none of the soft skills. Soft skills go hand in hand with hard talents, enabling your company to make the most of its technical competence.

✓ If you're great at attracting clients but not so great at keeping them, you probably have a soft skills gap.

✓ If you have a lot of staff turnover and have to retrain them all the time, you probably have a soft skills deficit.

### *There is a soft skills gap when there are many managers but no true leaders.*

An interpersonal dynamic in the job cannot be disregarded—listening, expressing ideas, resolving disagreement, and maintaining an open and honest work atmosphere all boil down to learning how to develop and manage interpersonal connections. People may actively participate in team efforts, show appreciation for others, and enlist support for their projects because of these ties.

It's critical that you acknowledge the critical function soft skills play within your team and try to improve them within yourself and throughout the organization.

## WHAT ARE THE BENEFITS OF SOFT SKILLS?

Soft skills may assist you, your team, and your company in a variety of ways, including:

- ✓ Increased productivity and efficiency
- ✓ Interpersonal and professional partnerships that are stronger
- ✓ More inventive solutions
- ✓ The expansion of the company

***Soft skills are valued by employers because they:***

Demonstrate initiative, proactivity, and self-assurance.

Assist them with comprehending your professional characteristics.

Determine if you are a good fit for a team and if your goals align with the organization.

Encourage a more positive corporate culture

Written and verbal communication skills are essential for most occupations since they enable you to engage effectively with all of the people you meet at work, such as clients, networkers, traders, and colleagues, and form solid relationships.

You must be able to communicate effectively across all platforms, including face-to-face, video calls, phone calls, and email. Having strong communication skills is a major benefit for any job in any field, and it is maybe the most crucial soft skill to develop. Strong written skills enable you to explain your goal clearly and concisely in e-mails, memos, and other written documents, ensuring that your bosses, colleagues, and clients are all on the same page.

Effective verbal communication allows you to set the tone in the company and foster relationships with coworkers and clients. The ability to interpret sophisticated insider discussion into understandable language is a valuable soft skill that can open doors to new prospects.

**There are three main types of communication skills that you can employ in your daily professional life:**

## VERBAL COMMUNICATION

Verbal communication entails conversing with anyone you meet at work, including persons at various levels of an organization. Interpersonal discussions, phone calls, public speaking, and effective communication with clients and customers, peers, and supervisors are examples of effective verbal communication.

## NONVERBAL COMMUNICATION

Understanding body language, maintaining good eye contact, managing your tone of voice and vocabulary, and using gestures to express involvement are all examples of nonverbal communication.

These skills are vital when giving presentations or working in particular areas, such as design, where digital visualization tools such as slide shows and movies are used.

## PARTS OF EFFECTIVE COMMUNICATION

Communication skills are necessary no matter what profession you have or how senior you are. When there is a breakdown in communication, efficiency, morale, and goals can all suffer as a result. Communication skills in the business world are highly sought after in today's competitive employment market, with recruiters searching for applicants that can communicate information, negotiate, and effectively deal with clients.

Listening intently, communicating effectively, and putting others at ease are all very desirable qualities.

### LISTEN WITHOUT INTERRUPTING

*Effective listening is the foundation of good communication.*

Active listening allows you to better focus on what a speaker is saying, retain more information, and confirm that you grasp their ideas, instructions, or wants, and expectations with follow-up questions.

Practice active listening by taking the time to listen to what the other person is saying.

Pay attention to what the other person is saying, ask questions to clarify points, and repeat what they've said to be sure you've got it right.

An attentive listener concentrates on whoever is saying. Active listeners rapidly win the respect of their coworkers, who value the time and attention given when speaking. As a result, the active listener may receive more attention in return. While it appears to be a basic skill, it can be difficult to master and improve. By focusing on the speaker and avoiding distractions, you can be an engaged listener. It's a good idea to follow up with questions, comments, or suggestions related to the chat topic.

When speaking, make sure you are clear and audible. This may not always imply yelling. You can be heard in a variety of situations by changing your speaking voice. This is a valuable talent that is necessary for good communication.

In some contexts, speaking excessively loudly can be perceived as impolite or arrogant. People will lose interest if they can't hear what you're saying if you speak too quietly. If you're unsure, observe how others communicate in the room.

The tone of your voice has the power to set the tone of a conversation. If you begin the conversation with an angry or unhelpful tone, the recipient is more likely to respond in kind. The level of emotion you use, the loudness you use, and the level of communication you choose all contribute to the tone of your voice.

The emphasis on certain words and the tone of your voice can give a statement a completely different interpretation. For example, in a customer complaint issue, your tone of voice should be as cool as possible, as a hostile tone would only exacerbate the situation.

## BODY LANGUAGE

Body language is used for a lot of communication. Facial expressions, eye contact, and the way someone sits are examples of nonverbal indicators. When you're listening to someone, please pay attention to both what they're saying and their nonverbal communication.

Don't slouch or fidget; instead, offer them your whole attention. Similarly, you should be aware of your own body language when talking to ensure that you're providing the right signals to others.

People are drawn to people who are confident. People are more inclined to respond to ideas provided by a confident speaker in the workplace. There are numerous techniques to project self-assurance. Consider making eye contact when chatting to someone or listening while sitting up straight with your shoulders open. Make sure you prepare ahead of time so that your ideas are polished and you can handle any queries that may arise. This will keep you from becoming agitated.

The ability to persuade is an important core talent. Employees with persuasive skills are valued in the workplace because they may influence a variety of areas of job performance. Furthermore, cooperation and leadership rely greatly on the capacity to persuade and influence people. Employees may not be as devoted to or sold on the importance of an organization's vision and long-term mission if they lack persuasion abilities.

We instantly identify persuasion with negative behavior when we think of it. Persuasion, on the other hand, can be used effectively to achieve our life objectives. Persuasion is the skill of persuading people to agree with your point of view or take a specific action. Persuasion is an intrinsic quality for some of us, and the ability to influence comes effortlessly. Persuasion skills can be learned and improved overtime for the rest of us.

## WHAT DOES IT MEAN TO HAVE PERSUASION SKILLS?

In simple terms, persuasion abilities are the capacity to make deliberate and successful attempts to influence someone through written or verbal communication. Simply described, persuasion abilities are the ability to change or influence someone's or a group's behaviors, beliefs, or attitudes toward another concept, person, or event. Reasoning, expressing feelings, and artfully delivering information are all common elements of persuasion.

## A FEW BASIC PERSUASION SKILLS

The key talents for effective persuasion are quite diverse. To begin with, great persuaders have high self-esteem and, more broadly, good Emotional Intelligence. They have a strong belief in their ability to succeed.

***You must also maintain your motivation and faith in yourself and your ideas.***

COMMUNICATION.

## COMMUNICATION.

Effective persuasion begins with effective communication. The most efficient technique to persuade others is to communicate with your coworkers because persuasion is a process that requires influencing others. Your message might be spoken, nonverbal, or both, but it must have an impact on your audience. They're more likely to listen to you if they engage with you.

## ACTIVE LISTENING

Understand someone's point of view on an issue before attempting to persuade them. It demonstrates patience and regards for others when you actively listen to them. Giving people the opportunity to express themselves makes them feel valued. This method of demonstrating your support will aid in the development of trust. You'll be able to understand better their motivations, which will help you develop persuasive arguments to earn their support.

Emotional intelligence is a talent that can help you communicate more effectively with your coworkers. You can answer appropriately if you can detect your listener's emotions. Adapt your persuasion strategies according to the situation.



Before you can convince someone to support your proposal, you must first convince them of its merits. In order to fully commit to your ideas or intentions, your listeners need to make a reasonable decision. To back up your plans, use logic and reasoning. If necessary, back them up with evidence. A graph or spreadsheet can help you better convey your logic. It can be used to make powerful arguments.



Persuasion abilities are built on your ability to communicate positively with others and build lasting relationships. You must be able to work in their best interests in order to maintain those relationships. When your coworkers thrive with you, they are more likely to agree with you. The more people accomplish and progress, the more credible you become.

Negotiation is a method of resolving disagreements and reaching agreements between two or more parties. Negotiations are commonplace in the workplace. Professionals may negotiate contract terms, project timeframes, salary, and other issues.

## WHAT DOES IT MEAN TO HAVE NEGOTIATION SKILLS?

Negotiation skills are characteristics that enable discourse between two or more people to resolve disputes. The fundamental goal of negotiating is to assist in the resolution of disagreements by achieving an agreement that is acceptable to all parties involved in a situation. Negotiation is typically a soft skill that combines qualities like analyzing, strategizing, persuasion, teamwork, and communication.

When you need to talk about anything, fight the impulse to worry about what you're going to say next as your partner speaks. Instead, pay attention to their ideas and then rephrase what you think they need to say to make sure you understand. Recognize any hard feelings lurking beneath the message, such as frustration. Not only are you likely to learn something useful, but the other party may try to imitate your excellent listening abilities.

## STRATEGIZING AND KNOWING YOUR WORTH

Your ability and desire to walk away and choose another agreement is your biggest source of power in both integrative and combative negotiations. Wise negotiators spend time defining their best alternative to a negotiated agreement and taking steps to improve it before approaching the bargaining table.

Wise negotiators work out the details of the procedure. When it comes to deciding when to meet, who should be present, what your objective will be, and so on, don't assume you're both on the same page. Instead, thoroughly plan out how you'll negotiate ahead of time. Such procedural difficulties will clear the way for far more detailed discussions.

The ability to analyze all possible outcomes of a situation and plan individual moves properly to avoid mistakes or failure is known as strategizing. Strategic thought and planning are the two most important aspects of strategizing. When used together, their main goal is to assist you in preparing for any event that may arise in the future.



The goals, interests, and opinions of both sides of the argument must be explained as a result of the conversation. It's a good idea to rank these elements in order of importance. It is frequently possible to identify or develop some common ground through this clarification.

Clarification is an important aspect of the negotiation process; without it, misunderstandings are likely to arise, posing issues and impediments to achieving a favorable conclusion.

## OFFER SOLUTION

Instead of making one offer at a time, consider making many bids at the same time. If your rival rejects them all, inquire as to which one he preferred and why. Then work on your own to improve the offer, or try to come up with a solution with the other party that will satisfy both of you. This method of proposing multiple offers at the same time reduces the chances of a deadlock and encourages more imaginative solutions.

## NEGOTIATE FOR A WIN-WIN SITUATION

This stage focuses on achieving a 'win-win' solution, in which both parties feel they have achieved something beneficial from the negotiating process and that their points of view have been taken into account. The optimum conclusion is usually a win-win situation. Although this may not always be achievable, it should be the ultimate goal of negotiation.

At this point, suggestions for alternate methods and compromises should be examined. Compromises are frequently beneficial options that can benefit all parties involved more than sticking to one's initial beliefs.

Relationships in the workplace can be quite useful to your professional success. Building solid professional relationships can aid in the acquisition of new talents as well as the application and development of existing ones. Because successful relationship-building often necessitates a combination of soft skills, it may be necessary to enhance these areas in order to advance in your job.

## WHAT DOES IT MEAN TO HAVE RELATIONSHIP-BUILDING SKILLS?

Relationship-building abilities are a set of soft talents used to connect with others and develop positive relationships. Relationship-building abilities are critical in the job for getting along with coworkers, contributing to a team, and establishing an understanding with others.

# HOW TO BUILD UP GOOD WORK RELATIONSHIPS?

## HELP OTHERS

Humans are sociable creatures by nature. And, given that we spend one-third of our lives at work, it's obvious that having strong relationships with our coworkers will make our jobs more enjoyable. The more at ease coworkers are with one another, the more confident they will be in expressing their opinions, brainstorming, and accepting new ideas, for example. To embrace change, create, and invent, this level of collaboration is required. When people see how well they can work together, group morale and productivity skyrocket.

You have more freedom when you have good working relationships rather than devoting time and energy to resolving a strained relationship.

## FIND COMMON INTEREST

Participating in various activities at your workplace is another approach to improve your relationship-building abilities. For example, you could meet up with a group of coworkers for coffee over lunch or attend an informal meeting to share your knowledge with your teammates.

You can develop your relationship-building skills by interacting with your coworkers and participating in various office events.

## ADD VALUE / GIVE RESPECT

Teams that work together with mutual respect recognize each other's contributions and develop solutions based on their joint wisdom, insight, and creativity. Self-awareness entails taking responsibility for your words and actions, as well as avoiding allowing your negative feelings to affect those around you.

Developing stronger professional relationships isn't always about proving you're better than others, despite what it may appear. In reality, being sympathetic to others, particularly those in subordinate positions to yours, will go a long way toward strengthening connections.

Rather than feeling smug because you accomplished something better or knew something that others didn't, turn the experience into a teaching opportunity and an

opportunity to help someone else.

At its most basic level, empathy is just being aware of other people's feelings and emotions. It is a crucial component of Emotional Intelligence, the relationship between self and others because it is how we as individuals comprehend what others are going through as if we were going through it ourselves.

Empathy is the ability to put yourself "in someone else's shoes accurately" – to understand the other person's position, thoughts, and feelings from their perspective – and express that knowledge back to them.

As a leader, you must be able to empathize with others. It helps you gain a better knowledge of your personnel, their perspectives, and their worries. It also improves your communication abilities because you can sense what other people want to know and whether or not they're getting it from you. Your employees should be able to develop empathy skills from you, which will help them become more effective leaders, managers, and supervisors.

Empathy is frequently confused with sympathy. However, the two are not synonymous. Sympathy is a feeling of caring for another person and a wish for them to be happier. Sympathy, unlike empathy, does not involve a shared point of view or emotions.

You can feel sympathy for someone in tears on the street, for example, even if you have no idea what their situation is. Sympathy can lead to empathy, although that isn't always the case.

## HOW TO BUILD UP EMPATHY SKILL

### TAKE AN INTEREST IN OTHER PEOPLE

Understanding the emotions of others is an important talent in the business. It has the potential to help us resolve problems, form more productive teams, and strengthen relationships with coworkers, clients, and customers.

However, while most of us are confident in our ability to learn new technical abilities, we may be unprepared to improve our interpersonal skills. And many people are uncomfortable discussing their own sentiments, let alone those of others!

## CONSIDER THE VIEWPOINTS OF OTHERS

You've probably heard the expression, "Walk a mile in their shoes before you judge them." Examine your own mindset and remain open-minded. Too much focus on one's own ideas and opinions leaves little room for empathy!

You may acknowledge what others think after you "see" why they believe it. This does not imply that you must agree with it; nonetheless, this is not the time for an argument. Instead, maintain a respectful demeanor and continue to listen.

There is no one-size-fits-all approach to demonstrating compassionate understanding. It will be determined by the situation, the individual, and their current dominating emotion. Remember that empathy is about what the other person wants and needs, not what you desire, so every action you do or recommend must benefit them.

For example, you may have a team member who is unable to concentrate on their work due to a personal issue. Telling them they can work from home until the matter is sorted may appear to be a nice gesture, but work may provide a welcome distraction from an unpleasant circumstance. As a result, ask them which approach they prefer.



And don't forget that empathy isn't just for crises! Seeing the world from multiple perspectives is a valuable skill that you can employ at any moment and in any situation. Random acts of kindness may make anyone's day better.

For instance, you probably smile and try to remember people's names: this is empathy in action. Empathic actions include paying full attention in meetings, being curious about people's lives and interests, and providing constructive feedback.



Pay attention to what someone is trying to say. To fully comprehend the message they're sending, use your ears, eyes, and "gut feelings."

- ✓ Start by paying attention to the essential words and phrases they employ, especially if they do so frequently.

- ✓ Then consider how they're saying it as well as what they're saying.

- ✓ What do their tone and body language say

- ✓ Are they enraged, embarrassed, or afraid?

Take it a step further by empathically listening. At this point, refrain from asking direct questions, arguing with what is being said, or disputing facts. Also, be adaptable —

expect the conversation to shift gears as the other person's

views and opinions evolve.

## OBSERVE THE MAJOR DIFFERENCES BETWEEN INDIVIDUALS.

People who have traveled or worked in multicultural

situations are one of the strongest examples of strong

empathy abilities. They've discovered that the way they

perceive and experience things differ from that of others.

People with limited or no empathy skills may be aware of

these discrepancies intellectually. However, until you have

experience with these variances, your empathy skills are

likely to be limited.

A positive attitude is more than just a happy smile; it has a lasting impact. Negative attitudes promote fear and a restriction of attention and mind, while positive attitudes promote the reverse. No one should be forced to live in a perpetual state of "fight or flight," but negative attitudes do just that.

It is reported having a genuine positive attitude makes your view of life appear broad and full of possibilities. That mindset leads to really living your life in a way that allows you to be exposed to and learn new talents on a regular basis.

## HOW TO DEVELOP A POSITIVE ATTITUDE

### STOP COMPLAINING

Complaining is ineffective. If you're in the company of people who whine a lot, get out of there. Try to see the situation from a new perspective. Complaints are a method of seeing things in a negative perspective and dismissing all alternative possibilities. It's a one-way street to disappointment that gets worse as you go.

Who you associate with has an impact on you. If you spend all of your time with negative people who moan about everything, you will eventually become a complainer and see the world through their eyes. You may believe that you would be able to change them by remaining positive, but this is not the case. Please make an effort to connect with people who enjoy their jobs, have fresh ideas, and are interested in a variety of things other than work. It will improve your entire viewpoint.

## KEEP YOUR WORDS IN CHECK.

This isn't about swearing less or the language police (although the latter is probably a good idea). It's all about being aware of the words you use when you talk and think.

The Sapir-Whorf hypothesis claims that the structure of language influences a person's perception of the world and their thinking. When taken to its logical conclusion, your language actually restricts or delimits your ability to see the world.

Granted, it's only a guess.

On a lesser scale, though, the language you use on a daily basis, both in your thoughts and in your spoken words, has a cumulative influence on how you think about yourself and your life.

This may appear to be a frivolous example, but it could be the difference between seeing your day as a series of tasks or as a series of chances. The former is exhausting and difficult, and it makes you feel like you're stuck in a rut. The latter has a lot of potential.

Be conscious of how you think and speak at work. Find a method to see everything and everyone in a positive light.

It makes you a joy to be kind to others. When it comes to happiness, doing something nice for others has the same effect as attempting new and exciting things.

What's better?

If you make being nice to others a habit, it will establish a cycle of generosity and happiness that will make you feel good while also making those around you feel good.

Consider the worst-case scenario for a bad work environment. Negativity grows on itself until it appears to be overwhelming. Be kind to others and watch them return the favor.

Employers seek candidates with outstanding teamwork abilities for a variety of reasons: they display leadership, collaboration, and good communication. Employees are expected to work as part of a team. Almost every industry, from business solutions to information technology to food services, needs teamwork.

## WHAT DOES IT MEAN TO HAVE TEAMWORK SKILLS?

Teamwork skills are a set of interconnected qualities that enable you to work with others in a structured and empathic manner in a variety of circumstances, meetings, and projects. Individuals who are mature and have good people skills are usually good at teamwork since it allows them to collaborate to attain the organization's goals.

## WHAT ARE THE BENEFITS OF HAVING GOOD TEAMWORK SKILLS?

In most organizations, teams exist in every department and division, which means that regardless of your industry or employment level, you will nearly always operate as part of a team. Working with team members in an empathic and responsible manner will help you reach your career goals, improve your CV, and assist the company to achieve its objectives.

Effective teamwork is also important for the team's success, morale, and employee retention. Teamwork abilities enable you to establish rapport with coworkers and other stakeholders, which can lead to deeper relationships, new network connections, and even new job chances. Teamwork also helps to a pleasant working atmosphere.

# HOW TO BUILD UP TEAMWORK SKILLS?

### AVOID CLAIMING ALL CREDIT

Even if just one person's name is on the project, in the corporate world, a good product is often the result of a team effort. Consider this: did you put together that fantastic sales presentation that landed you the big customer by yourself?

Most likely, you didn't. You may have presented the presentation, but who created the product, gathered data, conducted testing, devised a marketing strategy, and drafted the sales contract? It wasn't likely you; it was most likely a group of coworkers.

While most workplace triumphs are a team effort, the salesperson is the only one who receives a commission for bringing in a new client. That's fair because that's how the compensation structure is set up, and everyone agrees to it, but that doesn't mean the entire team shouldn't rejoice in their accomplishments.

Simply acknowledge that everyone on the team contributed to this success and that you will need their continued dedication to achieve actual success—a long-term satisfied customer.

Remember that the individual who gives the presentation and receives the credit is not always the same person who accomplished the effort behind the scenes. Managers have been known to take credit for work done by their employees. This is depressing and will most likely result in disgruntled staff.

***Don't forget to give credit where credit is due.***

## COLLABORATION

Working in a group might be difficult at times, but it's also a terrific way to come up with new ideas, share diverse viewpoints and experiences, and improve your own abilities. You may assist build a more productive team environment by treating each group project as a learning experience. Your eagerness to learn and try new things can help you become a better contributor, manager, or leader.

## GIVING GENUINE PRAISES

It is an excellent approach to show people warmth and support both at work and at home. You may show your thanks professionally at work by noticing the big and tiny ways people improve your environment. If you're in charge of a team, it's extremely crucial to recognize and thank your employees for their hard work.

Every employee wishes to know that they are doing a good job. Recognizing their qualities and abilities at work is an excellent method to increase their self-esteem. This could also lead to the continued success of your business. This compliment will go a long way if your teammate just finished a significant and difficult project.

Simply expressing "Thank you" can go a long way. It's enough to say, "You did a fantastic job." Offering this award in a public environment adds to the celebration and the employee's sense of accomplishment. Make your compliments as explicit as feasible and as quickly as possible. It's good to say things like, "You did a great job with that customer last week," but who are you talking about? If you can't express it right now, try giving details: "Do you recall the customer who complained about the thread count in the sheets?" You performed an excellent job of assisting her and ultimately persuading her to make a purchase."

## CELEBRATE SUCCESS

You are aware that you need to acknowledge and celebrate your achievements at work. When you celebrate your achievements on the job, it spawns greater success and increases your sense of fulfillment. For example, when a baby learns to walk, everyone gathers around and applauds each step the baby takes—even if half of them end with the baby plopping to the floor. People applaud the baby's progress and his determination to try again. You expect a lot of failure along the way, but it doesn't stop you from celebrating every victory.

Continuous, repetitive, or unglamorous tasks operate in the background of every firm. Take the time now and again to notice folks whose work is consistently excellent but rarely acknowledged. Demonstrate to them that their dependability and tenacity are not taken for granted.

These abilities can help you settle the conflict in a healthy manner and keep your relationships robust and thriving, regardless of the reason for arguments and disputes at home or work.

## WHAT IS THE CONFLICT?

Any healthy relationship will experience conflict at some point. After all, you can't expect two individuals to agree on everything all of the time. The goal is to learn how to resolve conflict in a healthy way rather than fearing or avoiding it.

When conflict is mismanaged, it may be devastating to a relationship, but disagreement can enhance the bond between two individuals when handled respectfully and positively. Learning these skills can help you resolve differences healthily and establish stronger, more fulfilling relationships, whether you're dealing with conflict at home, work, or school.

## HOW TO RESOLVE CONFLICT?

### COMMUNICATION

Employees must be able to communicate with one another to comprehend the source of conflict and opposing viewpoints—but communicating properly is more than just talking and getting your message across to others. Listening is an important part of effective communication. Employees that know how to use active listening tactics like asking questions, restating, and rephrasing remarks with analogies have a better chance of resolving the disagreement. The following are some other communication behaviors that aid in effective dispute resolution:

- ✓ Observing nonverbal signals

- ✓ Knowing when to speak up and when to be silent

✓ Explaining a concept or an opinion in a clear and simple manner



## AVOID ARGUMENTS

Individual personalities and disputes can frequently lead to team conflict. Individuals who understand the behaviors that lead to successful team functioning, on the other hand, can prevent and lessen workplace conflict. The following are some examples of behaviors that exhibit great teamwork abilities and aid in the resolution of workplace conflict:

Instead of focusing on differences, we should concentrate on common aims.

✓ Assuring that each team member has a clearly defined job might help to reduce conflicts over responsibilities.

✓ Putting one's own ego and desires aside and focusing on the needs of the rest of the team on a regular basis.

Problem-solving abilities promote conflict resolution by allowing people to approach a problem objectively and explore all of the possible answers. Individuals who know how to confront a problem rather than ignore or deny it can avoid or even lessen the likelihood of a conflict arising.

Individuals can adopt some particular problem-solving measures to resolve conflict in the workplace successfully. After identifying a dispute, it's a good idea to try to completely comprehend the source or reason of the problem before seeking to resolve it. Evaluation of numerous options and consideration of multiple interests are also important aspects of effective problem-solving.

## EMOTIONAL RESILIENCE

Workplace disagreement can elicit intense emotions, especially if the conflict makes a person feel that their job or position is in jeopardy. As a result, emotional agility is a crucial conflict resolution skill since it helps one to comprehend the emotions of all parties involved in a disagreement, including one's own. Putting oneself in another's shoes and developing empathy and compassion is also part of being emotionally aware.

Leadership development can assist in the development of emotional agility as well as provide important skills for successfully resolving conflict. It can, for example, teach people how to master persuading tactics and how to leverage relationships.

Emotional intelligence (EQ) is the ability to recognize, use, and control one's own emotions in a constructive way in order to reduce stress, communicate effectively, sympathize with others, overcome obstacles, and diffuse conflict. Emotional intelligence aids in the development of stronger relationships, academic and professional success, and the attainment of career and personal objectives. It can also assist you in connecting with your emotions, putting your intentions into action, and making educated decisions about what is most important to you.

## IS EMOTIONAL INTELLIGENCE (EQ) A SOFT SKILL?

Emotional intelligence, interpersonal abilities, and social skills are sometimes lumped together. For one thing, they're intangible, but they have a huge impact on practically everything we do. These are all soft skills that a skilled therapist may readily assist you with.

At the same time, the term "soft skill" does not imply that interpersonal abilities like EI cannot be tested psychometrically or that they cannot be developed in highly effective ways by the individual.

## HOW TO BUILD EMOTIONAL INTELLIGENCE

### SELF-AWARENESS

Self-awareness includes the following:

- ✓ Emotional intelligence
- ✓ Accurate self-evaluation
- ✓ Self-confidence

Self-awareness is the ability to recognize and understand your emotions as they arise and change. It is incorrect to categorize emotions as positive or negative. Instead of thinking of them as inappropriate, think of them as appropriate or acceptable.

Anger, for example, is typically thought of as a negative emotion. However, it can be a perfectly acceptable and healthy emotion in certain circumstances — emotional intelligence allows us to recognize our anger and understand why it has arisen.

Self-evaluation of moods and emotions might help you develop.

## SELF-REGULATION

How you manage your emotions, behaviors, and impulses is referred to as self-regulation. The easier this becomes, the more self-aware you are; if you can recognize what you're experiencing and why you'll be able to respond correctly.

Self-management skills are concerned with how well you regulate your emotions at any given time or in any given situation. Self-control is an important component of this, but there are other factors to consider, such as whether you conduct in a way that is considered to be "good" or "virtuous."

✓ ***Allowing Time to Pause and Think Before Responding***

Allow yourself time to pause and think before responding. It could be as simple as taking a deep breath and pausing for 20 seconds to let your sensations to overtake your mind.

✓ ***Taking a Step Back***

It's fine if you need to leave the room from time to time. Taking a walk, drinking some water, or calling a buddy is often preferable to making a quick decision, sending a caustic email, or lashing out at your colleagues.

✓ ***Recognizing Your Emotions***

Make a list of how you're feeling and what's causing your distress. You'll most likely begin to notice patterns. You'll be more prepared the next time a comparable situation arises if you know what triggers you.

Empathy, or the ability to comprehend how others feel, is an essential component of emotional intelligence. However, it entails more than merely being able to perceive others' emotional states.

It also includes how you respond to others based on the information you've gathered.

- ✓ How do you react when you think someone is depressed or hopeless?

You may show them more tenderness and concern, or you could make an attempt to lift their spirits. Empathy also permits you to comprehend the power dynamics that frequently influence social connections, particularly in the workplace. This is crucial for steering your interactions with the various people you meet on a daily basis.

Being able to manage your time efficiently can help you increase your productivity. You can arrange your daily workload and prepare for meetings with excellent time management abilities. These abilities also enable you to meet deadlines for your deliverables.

## WHAT EXACTLY ARE TIME-MANAGEMENT ABILITIES?

Time-management abilities are those that enable you to organize your time in order to be more productive properly. Learning to manage your time successfully will enhance your career because time-management skills are transferable skills that can be applied to any job.

Time management is described as the ability to use your time productively and efficiently—but what if you're working as efficiently as possible but still can't get everything done?

Working effectively and prioritizing your time may be a better way to think about time management.

To put it another way, those who are skilled at time management are also good at getting things done. They are, however, better at prioritizing and determining what truly has to be done—and then dismissing the rest.



Make a list of tasks that require immediate attention before you begin your day. Unimportant jobs can eat up a lot of your time, and we often give them too much of our attention because they are easier or less stressful.

Identifying important jobs that must be finished that day, on the other hand, is critical to your productivity. Once you've figured out where to focus your energy, you'll be able to get things done in a way that suits you and your schedule.

Set a realistic deadline and stick to it when you have a task to do. Once you've set a deadline, it's a good idea to jot it down on a sticky note and keep it near your desk. This will serve as a visual reminder to stay on track.

Set a deadline a few days before the assignment is due so you can do all of the other projects that may come up. Challenge yourself and stick to the deadline; congratulate yourself on completing a challenging task.



If you believe you are already overworked, politely decline extra assignments. Before committing to take on additional work, have a look at your to-do list.

Many people fear that saying no would make them appear ungrateful, but the truth is that saying no is one of the most effective strategies to prioritize your time and self-care. When you take care of this, you'll discover that you have more energy to dedicate to the things that matter, which your friends and family will enjoy.

## TAKE BREAKS FREQUENTLY

Take a 10- to 15-minute rest if you feel tired or agitated. Stress can have a negative impact on your health and productivity.

Even better, set out time for your breaks. It allows you to unwind and return to work with renewed vigor. If you know a break is on the way, you'll be more inclined to push through boredom or a lack of enthusiasm to complete the task at hand.

Take a walk, listen to music, or stretch for a few minutes. The greatest option is to take a complete break from work and spend time with friends and family.

In the workplace, work ethic is important.

Employers search for applicants who have a strong work ethic. A strong work ethic allows you to concentrate on duties, act professionally, persevere in difficult situations, and show responsibility and dependability in the workplace. People who have a high work ethic are often better employees than those who do not, and hiring managers will frequently choose candidates with a strong work ethic over those who do not.

## WHAT IS A WORK ETHIC

A person's work ethic is a term used to define their commitment to their employment. While every employee may show up to work and do their obligations, not everyone possesses a strong work ethic that enables them to place a high value on their professional life and achievement and commit to doing everything it takes to complete the task.

Employers value employees with good work ethic skills because they demonstrate drive and devotion to their function within the firm. Hard work is a natural aspect of the job for those with a strong work ethic, and they aren't intimidated by the need to put in the effort to succeed in the workplace.

## WHAT WORK ETHICS COMPRISES?

### DEPENDABILITY AND RESPONSIBILITY

Employers respect individuals who arrive on time. It's critical to keep professionals informed of schedule changes or if you'll be late for any reason. This also entails keeping your management informed about all of your assigned projects. Being dependable and responsible as an employee demonstrates to your employer that you respect your job and are also accountable for staying on top of tasks and keeping them informed about important information.

Employers look for self-motivated applicants who require little command and direction to do tasks in a timely and professional manner. Managers who hire self-motivated employees are doing themselves a great favor. Employees who are self-motivated require less guidance from their superiors. When a self-motivated individual knows their job responsibilities, they will complete them without the assistance of others.

## HONESTY AND INTEGRITY

When working for a company, an employer wants to know that they can trust what you say and do. Successful firms endeavor to earn consumers' trust and maintain the belief that the customer is always right. It is each individual's responsibility to apply their moral and ethical sense when working with and supporting others within the scope of their job.

People with a high work ethic arrive on time, complete the assigned work on time, and follow through on their commitments. Notify your boss if you are going to be late for work. Let your team know if you won't be able to complete a job on time. If you need assistance, ask for it, and if you say you'll do something, follow-through, even if you don't want to. Being dependable demonstrates to your employer that you value your employees and will complete projects and responsibilities as allocated.



Employees with a strong work ethic conduct themselves professionally in all aspects of their jobs. Professionalism is defined as a person's commitment to conduct themselves professionally in terms of how they dress, speak, and show themselves. It also refers to a person's commitment to mastering every part of their job and performing to their full potential at work.

People with a strong work ethic can stay concentrated on a task for as long as it takes to complete it. You can basically train yourself to work for longer periods of time while simultaneously working harder if you develop tenacity. To avoid burnout, it's necessary to strike a balance between perseverance and proper relaxation. When it comes to work ethics, the focus is just as crucial as perseverance. You'll be able to finish chores faster and avoid distractions if you focus.

# CONCLUSION

Soft skills are features, traits, innate social cues, and communicative skills that can translate to success in a given profession. They are defined by how a person interacts with people in the workplace.

Soft talents are more comparable to emotions or insights than hard skills, which are more easily learned. They are difficult to assess and quantify, but they are appealing to businesses because most occupations require employees to communicate with one another. Showing that you're capable of this engagement may take some time, but soft skills are inherently transferable and adaptable so that they may be used in any profession.

While it is critical to demonstrate to your employer that you are prepared to put in long hours, it is also critical to strike a healthy work-life balance. When you work too much, you may become overwhelmed and begin to sabotage your job.

It is critical to get enough sleep and to take the time necessary to refresh and relax.

It is simple to establish a strong soft skills that employers and coworkers will value if you are motivated. By having this great soft skills, it may help you to get the promotion, to get new employment, and have other favorable results that you want.

## REFERENCE

https://www.mbaskool.com/business-concepts/human-resources-hr-terms/1779-career-development.html

https://www.mindtools.com/pages/article/newCDV_34.htm

https://uk.indeed.com/career-advice/career-development/communication-skills

https://www.skillsyouneed.com/ips/communication-skills.html

https://harappa.education/harappa-diaries/persuasion-skills/

https://www.skillsyouneed.com/ips/persuasion-skills.html

https://www.mindtools.com/pages/article/newCDV_34.htm

https://uk.indeed.com/career-advice/career-development/negotiation-skills

https://www.pon.harvard.edu/daily/negotiation-skills-daily/top-10-negotiation-skills/

https://www.skillsyouneed.com/ips/negotiation.html

https://www.mindtools.com/pages/article/good-relationships.htm

https://gethppy.com/workplace-happiness/building-professional-relationships

https://www.mindtools.com/pages/article/EmpathyatWork.htm

https://www.skillsyouneed.com/ips/empathy.html

https://wheniwork.com/blog/18-simple-ways-to-keep-a-positive-attitude-at-work

https://positivepsychology.com/positive-mindset/

https://www.leapsome.com/blog/how-to-celebrate-success-at-work

https://www.thebalancecareers.com/how-to-celebrate-success-at-work-4160403

https://zety.com/blog/teamwork-skills

https://www.herzing.edu/blog/7-important-teamwork-skills-you-need-school-and-your-career

https://www.thebalancecareers.com/list-of-teamwork-skills-2063773

https://uk.indeed.com/career-advice/career-development/teamwork-skills

https://www.helpguide.org/articles/relationships-communication/conflict-resolution-skills.htm

https://www.eaglesflight.com/blog/top-5-skills-needed-to-successfully-resolve-conflicts-in-the-workplace

https://online.hbs.edu/blog/post/emotional-intelligence-skills

https://www.skillsyouneed.com/general/emotional-intelligence.html

https://www.verywellmind.com/components-of-emotional-intelligence-2795438

https://uk.indeed.com/career-advice/career-development/time-management-skills

https://www.skillsyouneed.com/ps/time-management.html

https://www.glassdoor.com/blog/guide/work-ethic-skills/

https://www.gptc.edu/compliance-notices/work-ethics/